SING ALONG COWBOY!

SING ALONG COWBOY!

Songs of the Wild Frontier

Rich Hinrichsen

Published by Rich Hinrichsen
P.O. BOX 31378
Seattle, WA 98103
rich@tangocowboys.com
www.tangocowboys.com

ISBN 9781797741536

To my Montana relatives who are singers, chiropractors, cowboys, and cattle ranchers.

Acknowledgements

The author gratefully acknowledges Rob Quist, Rosy Betz-Zall, Tom Bourne, Steve Peha, and Catherine Hinrichsen for their help in preparing this book for publication.

Contents

Foreword by Rob Quist

When I first began playing banjo, and had learned enough chords to play with other musicians, my greatest pleasure was to attend the hootenannies that were so prevalent during that era. There was something incredibly magical, being with friends playing lively renditions throughout the evening, as well as the sweet, mellow songs as the event began winding down. Our favorite cowboy songs, then and now, are representations of one of the most colorful periods of our nation's history and since many of them were based on melodies of folk songs from countries that our ancestors immigrated from, they have become deeply imprinted in our DNA. One little known fact, is that the first record to sell a million copies in America was the wonderful cowboy song by D. J. O'Malley called "When the Work's All Done This Fall." Even today, it remains as one of my favorites.

Michael Martin Murphey, arguably the present day standard bearer for these classic songs of our heritage, went to great lengths to convince his record company to release an album of traditional cowboy songs, because he knew that there was an appreciation for them that ran deep and wide throughout the country. His first release was so popular and successful that Warner Brothers subsequently created a whole new subsidiary called Warner Western to record and promote a whole series of his cowboy songs compilations, as well as those of other artists who love and perform this truly American music. Murphey has released several such albums in recent years, and I have had the great honor of co-writing several original songs for these projects with him.

Countless times I have been invited to guest ranches to sing around campfires for attendees who want to share in the Western experience, and I believe that Rich Hinrichsen's book *Sing Along Cowboy!* will be invaluable for those who want to vocalize more than just one remembered verse and chorus. I have always believed that music is for everyone to share, not just performers, and we now know that the benefits of participating in music can be life changing. Recent studies have shown that singing together as a group raises endorphin levels and promotes bonding, something which is sorely needed in today's world.

So, flip through these pages, take a journey through the musical history of America, and let the music carry you away.

Introduction

Although the great cattle drives of the American West are long past, the American cowboy is alive and well and continues to be celebrated in film, theatre, and song. Thanks to the efforts of collectors such as John and Alan Lomax, Jack Thorp, Carl Sandburg, and others, the songs from the cowboy's heyday live on and are sung today. In this little collection, you can hear songs about horses, cow punchers, outlaws, and prospectors. These songs are little comedies and tragedies of the open range—songs written by cowboys and others to entertain their friends with factual and fraudulent stories of the free, but lonely life of a cowboy.

Before radio, television, and the internet, entertainment consisted of a handful of friends or relatives gathering at a store, a barn, a campfire, or a neighbor's house to dance, tell stories, and sing and play together. Many of those old songs are lengthy compared to recordings of today, perhaps because singing them was so much fun that no one wanted them to end, so the verses multiplied. The pop song with its 3-5 minute format didn't exist in the 1800s; it was an invention made necessary in the early 20th century by the limited capacity of the 78 r.p.m. flat disc record.

These great cowboy songs are not like family photos to be placed upon the mantle and admired; instead they are living things meant to be sung. In the age of the internet, as people become more isolated, they long to connect face-to-face with others. Meetings of friends and family over a song can strengthen bonds and create a sense of well-being. Good old communal singing is alive and well today, and opportunities abound in choirs, churches, fellowship halls, song circles, camps, and sing-alongs.

This book is made for folks who want to come together over a song. Peruse the table of contents to find gems like "Cowboy's Lament," (a.k.a. "Streets of Laredo"), or "Cielito Lindo" —with its catchy lyrics "*Ay, Ay, Ay, canta no llores*"—and the famous "Home on the Range." These songs will transport you to another time and place. You may find yourself playing a role in the song: the boss, the outlaw, the broken cowboy, the lonely lass, the valiant buckaroo, the sheriff, the loyal friend, brother, sister, father, or the mourning mother. Switch roles from verse to verse, chorus to chorus, or song to song, living life through someone else's eyes. Bring your prairie dress, your cowboy hat, your jeans, your horse, your flannel shirt, but best of all, bring your voice, and grab a pal or two.

Several of these songs are written in Spanish. This is fitting given that the cowboy owes much to the *vaquero* of Spanish America. *Vaquero* is derived from the Spanish word *vaca*, meaning "cow." When the cattle herds of the Spanish missions grew too large for the priests to handle by themselves, indigenous peoples were recruited (enslaved) as horsemen to assist. By the 1700s, *vaqueros* were of mixed Spanish and indigenous background (The Metropolitan Museum of Art 1991). The ballad "Corrido de Kansias" ("Ballad of Kansas") was composed by Texas Mexican cowboys during the cattle drives of the 1860s. The song is presented in two of its variations, "Corrido de Kansias I" and "Corridor de Kansias II," stories of death, heroism, and Mexican pride. Also included are beloved Mexican folk songs "Cielito Lindo" ("Lovely Sweet One"), "La Cucaracha" ("The Cockroach"), and others.

This collection does not contain the cowboy songs penned for the film industry, such as "Back In The Saddle Again," "Tumbling Tumbleweeds," "Ghost Riders In The Sky," "Don't Fence Me In," and "Cool Water." Although these songs are treasures, they are not yet in the public domain. For a wonderful collection of Hollywood's cowboy songs, see Jim Bob Tinsley's *For A Cowboy Has To Sing* (1991). In the spirit of Hollywood's cowpuncher songs, I've included my own song, "Yipeetyee I'm off to Truckee," which is the story of a buckaroo with sixteen gold pieces in his purse, who tries to reach his sweetheart in Truckee, California, but is imperiled when snow comes early to the Sierra Nevada.

You might say, "Well, I'm not a cowboy, and I'd feel inauthentic singing those songs." In *American Songbag* (1927), Carl Sandburg wrote,

"There is something authentic about any person's way of giving a song which has been known, lived with and loved, for many years, by the singer."

In other words, authentic cowboy singing is possible for anyone; all that's required is a love for the songs and persistence. Live with and sing these songs for years to discover the truth and beauty in these miniature Shakespearean dramas, and the singing itself will grow true and beautiful. Regardless of your country of origin or background, authentic American cowboy singing is within your grasp. Sing out!

Sing the Cowboy Way

There is no single "cowboy way" of singing a song: every person brings something unique to a song, and that's part of what makes singing fun. However, there are a few tricks of the trade—picked up by experience, instruction, and observation—that will come in handy if you want to connect with others and preserve your voice for the next song. Follow this advice and you might get smiles from your comrades and perhaps an extra helping of beans from the trail drive cook.

Sing like you speak. Emphasize the meanings of words and let them roll off your tongue as simply as if you were chatting to a neighbor, telling a bed time story to your son or daughter, yelling at the referee, calling your dog, or whispering sweet nothings to the one you love.

Relax completely. Singing is an athletic undertaking. As any superb athlete would do, only engage the muscles necessary for the task. It's best to relax your throat and face completely and let the real powerhouse—your lungs—take control, but without force. The air is to singing as the bow is to playing the violin. Caress your vocal cords with your breath like you would a canary—not a horse! Breathe in deeply and take a breath when your air feels low. To relax the tongue, try using "lazy diction," as if your tongue were filled with novocaine. With the tongue relaxed, the air can flow from your lungs, through your vocal cords, and out of your mouth unencumbered, creating a resonant sound. Now, with your tongue nice and floppy, add good diction back into your singing.

Know who you are singing to. Visualize who you are singing to and your voice will carry and project the right emotion. Emotion is not dredged up from looking inward; instead emotion comes naturally by paying attention to who you are singing to (the target). Direct your air, your thoughts, and attention to your target, and the emotion will be there. Singing a note is a lot like pitching a horseshoe—use too much effort and you overshoot; too little, and you undershoot; just what is needed and the horseshoe hits the metal stake with a glorious ring. To get that ring with your voice, use just the air that is needed to reach the target: no more and no less.

COWBOY SONGS

EL ABANDONADO

ACROSS THE WIDE MISSOURI

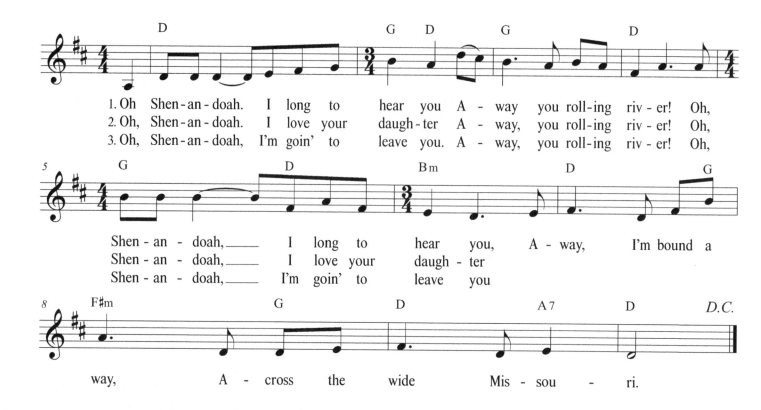

1. Oh Shen - an - doah. I long to hear you A - way you roll-ing riv - er! Oh,
2. Oh, Shen - an - doah. I love your daugh-ter A - way, you roll-ing riv - er! Oh,
3. Oh, Shen - an - doah, I'm goin' to leave you. A - way, you roll-ing riv - er! Oh,

Shen - an - doah,_____ I long to hear you, A - way, I'm bound a
Shen - an - doah,_____ I love your daugh - ter
Shen - an - doah,_____ I'm goin' to leave you

way, A - cross the wide Mis - sou - ri.

THE BIG CORRAL

3. The wrangler's out a-combing the hills.
   Press along to the Big Corral.
   So jump in your britches and grease up your gills.
   Press along to the Big Corral.
   (Chorus)

4. The chuck we get ain't fit to eat.
   Press along to the Big Corral.
   There's rocks in the beans and sand in the meat.
   Press along to the Big Corral.
   (Chorus)

4

BILLY THE KID

1. I'll sing you a true song of Bil - ly the
2. When Bil - ly the Kid was a ver - y young
3. Fair Mex - i - can maid - ens play gui - tars and

Kid; I'll sing of the des - per - ate deeds that he
lad, In old Sil - ver Ci - ty he went to the
sing A song a - bout Bil - ly, their boy ban - dit

did Way out in New Mex - i - co long, long a -
bad. Way out in the West with his gun in his
king. How ere his young man - hood had reached its sad

go, When a man's on - ly chance was his own for - ty - four.
hand, At the age of twelve years____ he killed his first man.
end, He'd a notch on his pis - tol for twen - ty - one men.

4. 'Twas on the same night when poor Billy died,
   He said to his friends, "I am not satisfied;
   There are twenty-one men I have put bullets through,
   And sheriff Pat Garrett will make twenty-two."

5. Now this is how Billy the Kid met his fate:
   The bright moon was shining, the hour was late,
   Shot down by Pat Garrett, who once was his friend.
   The young outlaw's life had now come to an end.

6. There's many a man with a face fine and fair,
   Who starts out in life with a chance to be square.
   But just like poor Billy, he wanders astray,
   And loses his life in the very same way.

BLOOD ON THE SADDLE

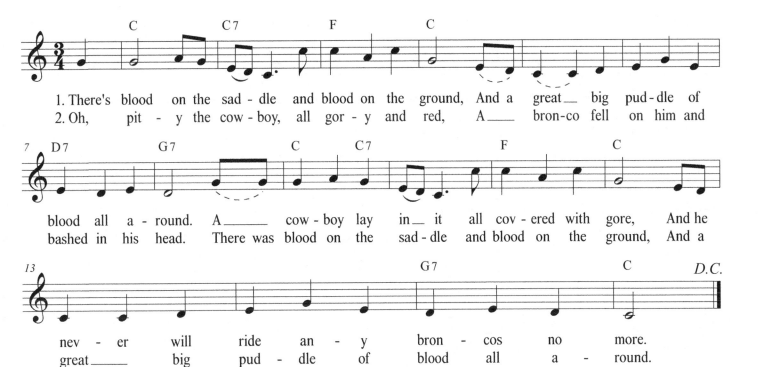

1. There's blood on the sad - dle and blood on the ground, And a great___ big pud - dle of
2. Oh, pit - y the cow - boy, all gor - y and red, A___ bron-co fell on him and

blood all a - round. A_____ cow - boy lay in___ it all cov - ered with gore, And he
bashed in his head. There was blood on the sad - dle and blood on the ground, And a

nev - er will ride an - y bron - cos no more.
great_____ big pud - dle of blood all a - round.

6
BUFFALO GALS

1. As I was walk-in' down the street, Down the street, down the street, A
2. I asked her if she'd have a dance, Have a dance, care to dance. I
3. I asked that gal to be my wife, Be my wife, be my wife. I'd

pret - ty lit - tle girl I chanced to meet, Oh, she was fair to see.
thought__ that__ I might get a chance To shake a foot with her.
be so ver - y hap - py all my life If she were by my side.

Buf - fa - lo gals, won't you come out to-night? Come out to-night? Come out to-night?

Buf - fa - lo gals, won't you come out to-night And dance by the light of the moon?

THE BUFFALO HUNTERS

1. Oh, come___ all you pret - ty fair maids, these lines to you I
2. Our game it is the an - te - lope, the buf - f'lo, elk, and

write:___ We're go - ing on the range___ in which we take de -
deer.___ They roam the broad prai - ries___ with - out the least of

light.___ We're go - ing on the range,___ as we poor hunt - ers
fear.___ We rob them of their robes,___ in which we think no

do,___ So those ten - der - foot - ed fel - lows__ can stay at home with you.__
harm,___ To buy us chuck and cloth-ing__ to keep our bod - ies warm.

3. The buffalo is the largest and the noblest of the band.
He sometimes refuses to throw us up his hand.
His shaggy main thrown forward, his head raised to the sky,
He seems to say, "We're coming, boys, so hunter, mind your eye!"

4. It's all of the day long as we go tramping 'round
In search of the buff'lo that we may shoot him down;
Our guns upon our shoulders, our belts of forty rounds,
We send them up Salt River to their happy hunting grounds.

5. Our fires are made of mesquite roots, our beds are on the ground;
Our houses made of buffalo hides, we make them tall and round;
Our furniture is the camp kettle, the coffee pot, and pan,
Our chuck it is both bread and meat, mingled well with sand.

BURY ME NOT ON THE LONE PRAIRIE

1. "Oh, bur-y me not _____ on the lone prai - rie." _____ These ___ words came
2. "Oh, bur-y me not _____ on the lone prai - rie," _____ Where the coy - otes

low _____ and ___ mourn - ful - ly _____ From the pal - lid lips _____
howl _____ and the wind blows free, _____ In a nar - row grave, _____

___ of a youth who lay _____ On his dy - ing bed _____ at the close of
___ just six by three. _____ Oh, ___ bur-y me not _____ on the lone prai -

D.C. for additional verses

day. _____
rie." _____

After last verse

"Oh, bur-y me not _____ on the lone prai - rie.... _____ Oh, bur-y me not _____

___ on the lone prai - rie..." _____

3. "It matters not, often I've been told,
   Where the body lies when the heart grows cold.
   Yet grant, oh grant, this wish to me:
   Oh, bury me not on the lone prairie."

4. "I've always wished to be laid when I died
   In the little churchyard on the green hillside.
   By my father's grave there let mine be,
   And bury me not on the lone prairie."

5. "Let my death sleep be where my mother's pray'r
   And a sister's tear will mingle there.
   Where friends can come and weep o'er me.
   Oh, bury me not on the lone prairie."

6. "Oh, bury me not on the lone prairie,
   Where the wolves can howl and growl o'er me.
   Fling a handful of roses o'er my grave,
   With a pray'r to Him who my soul will save."

7. "Oh, bury me not..." and his voice failed there,
   But we took no heed of his dying pray'r.
   In a narrow grave, just six by three,
   We buried him there on the lone prairie.

8. And cowboys now as they roam the plain,
   For they marked the spot where his bones were lain,
   Fling a handful of roses o'er his grave
   With a pray'r to God, his soul to save.

CHOPO

1. Through__ rock - y a - rro - yos__ so dark and so deep, Down the
2. Wheth - er sin - gle or dou - ble or the lead of a team, O - ver

sides of the moun - tains so slip - p'ry and steep, You've good judg - ment, sure - foot - ed wher-
high - ways or by - ways or cross - ing a stream, You're__ al - ways in fix__ and

e - ver you go; You're a safe - ty con - vey - ance, my lit - tle Cho - po.
will - ing to go, When - ev - er you're called on, my *chi - co* Chop - o.

3. You're a good roping horse;
    you were never jerked down.
   When tied to a steer,
    you will circle him round.
   Let him once cross the string,
    and over he'll go.
   You *sabe* the business,
    my cow horse Chopo.

4. One day on the Llano,
    A hailstorm began.
   The herds were stampeded;
    the horses all ran.
   The lightning, it glittered,
    a cyclone did blow,
   But you faced the sweet music,
    my little Chopo.

CIELITO LINDO

CINDY

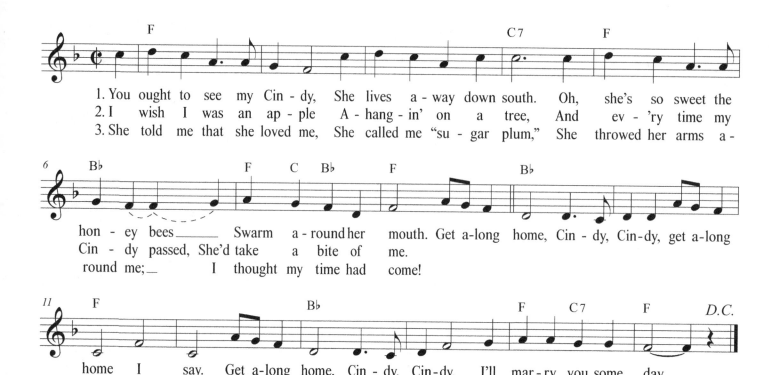

1. You ought to see my Cin - dy, She lives a - way down south. Oh, she's so sweet the
2. I wish I was an ap - ple A - hang - in' on a tree, And ev - 'ry time my
3. She told me that she loved me, She called me "su - gar plum," She throwed her arms a -

hon - ey bees_____ Swarm a - round her mouth. Get a - long home, Cin - dy, Cin - dy, get a - long
Cin - dy passed, She'd take a bite of me.
round me;___ I thought my time had come!

home I say. Get a - long home, Cin - dy, Cin - dy, I'll mar - ry you some day.___

4. I wish I had a needle,
   As fine as I could sew,
   I'd sew that gal to my coattail
   And down the road I'd go.
   (Chorus)

5. Cindy in the springtime,
   Cindy in the fall,
   If I can't have my Cindy,
   I'll have no girl at all.
   (Chorus)

THE COLORADO TRAIL

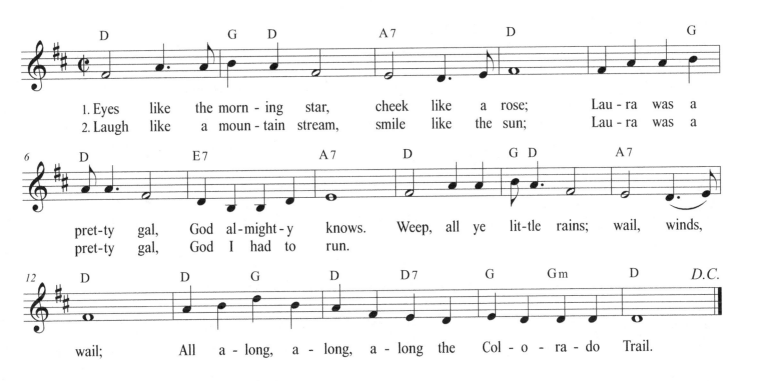

1. Eyes like the morn - ing star, cheek like a rose; Lau - ra was a
2. Laugh like a moun - tain stream, smile like the sun; Lau - ra was a

pret-ty gal, God al-might-y knows. Weep, all ye lit-tle rains; wail, winds,
pret-ty gal, God I had to run.

wail; All a - long, a - long, a - long the Col - o - ra - do Trail.

CORRIDO DE KIANSIS I

1. Cuan - do sal - i - mos pa' Kian - sis_____ con un -
2. Nos dec - ía_el_____ ca - po - ral,_____ co - mo
3. ¡Ah, qué cam - i - no tan bue - no!_____ to - do

a gran - de part - i - da,_____ ¡ah qué cam - i - no tan
quer - ien - do llor - ar:_____ A - llá va la nov - i -
se le i - ba_en cor - er, _____ ¡y,_ah, que fuer - te_a -

lar - go! no con - ta - ba con la vi - da._____
lla - da, no me la de - jen_____ pa - sar._____
gua - ce - ro! no con - ta - ba yo_en volv - er._____

4. Unos pedían un cigatto,
   otros pedían que comer,
   y el caporal nos decía:
   Sea por Dios, qué hemos de hacer.

5 En el charco de Palomas
   se cortó un novillo bragado,
   y el caporal lo lazó
   en su caballo melado.

6. Avísenle al caporal
   que un vaquero se mató,
   en las trancas del corral
   nomás la cuera dejó.

7. Llegamos al Río Salado
   y nos tiramos a nado,
   decía un americano:
   Esos hombres ya se ahogaron.

8. Puese qué pensaría ese hombre
   que venimos a esp'rimentar,
   si somos del Río Grande,
   de los buenos pa' nadar.

9. Y le dimos vista a Kiansis,
   y nos dice el caporal:
   Ora sí somos de la vida,
   ya vamos a hacer corral.

10. De vuelta en San Antonio
    compramos buenos sombreros,
    y aquí se acaban cantando
    versos de los aventureros.

CORRIDO DE KIANSIS II

1. Cuan - do sal - i - mos pa' Kian - sis ____ con un -
   a gran - de cor - ri - da, ____ grit - a - ba mi ca - por -
   al: ____ Les en - carg - o a mi quer - i - da. ____

2. Con - test - a ot - ro ca - por - al: ____ No ten -
   gas cui - da - do, es so - la; que la mu - jer que es hon -
   ra - da ____ aun - que vi - va en - tre la bo - la. ____

3. Qui - nien - tos no - vi - llos e - ran, ____ to - dos
   gran - des y li - vian - os, ____ y en - tre trein - ta a - mer - i -
   can - os ____ no los po - dían em - ba - lar. ____

4. Llegan cinco mexicanos,
   todos bien enchivarrados,
   y en menos de un cuarto de hora
   los tenían encerrados.

5. Esos cinco mexicanos
   al momento los echaron,
   y los treinta americanos
   se quedaron azorados.

6. Los novillos eran bravos,
   no se podían soportar,
   gritaba un Americano:
   Que se baje el caporal.

7. Pero el caporal no quiso
   y un vaquero se arrojó;
   a que lo matara el toro,
   nomás a eso se bajó.

8. La mujer de Alberto Flores
   le pregunta al caporal:
   Déme usted razón de mi hijo,
   que no lo he visto llegar.

9. Señora, yo le diría,
   pero se pone a llorar;
   lo mató un toro fortino
   en las trances de un corral.

10. Ya con ésta me despido
    por 'l amor de mi querida,
    ya les canté a mis amigos
    los versos de la corrida.

COWBOY JACK

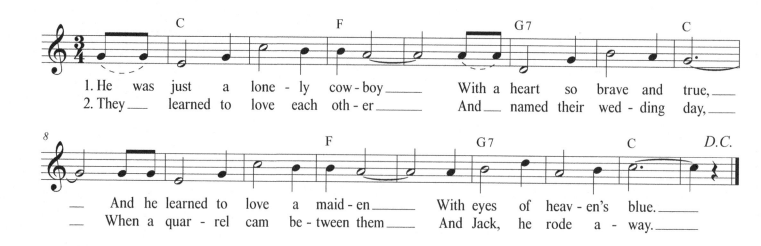

1. He was just a lone - ly cow-boy___ With a heart so brave and true,___
2. They___ learned to love each oth - er___ And___ named their wed - ding day,___

___ And he learned to love a maid - en___ With eyes of heav - en's blue.___
___ When a quar - rel cam be - tween them___ And Jack, he rode a - way.___

3. He joined a band of cowboys,
   And tried to forget her name,
   But out on the lonesome prarie
   She waits for him the same.

4. One night when work was finished,
   Just at the close of day,
   Someone said, "Sing a song, Jack,
   To drive dull cares away."

5. When Jack began his singing,
   His mind did wander back,
   For he sang of a maiden
   Who waited for her Jack.

6. "Your sweetheart waits for you, Jack;
   Your sweetheart waits for you,
   Out on the lonesome prarie
   Where the skies are always blue."

7. Jack left the camp next morning
   Breathing his sweetheart's name.
   I'll go and ask forgiveness,
   For I know that I'm to blame."

8. But when he reached the prairie
   He found a new-made mound.
   And his friends they sadly told him
   They'd laid his loved one down.

9. They said as she lay dying
   She breathed her sweetheart's name,
   And asked them with her last breath
   To tell him when he came:

10. "Your sweetheart waits for you, Jack:
    Your sweetheart waits for you,
    Out on the lonesome prairie
    Where the skies are always blue."

COWBOY LULLABY

1. Des-ert sil-ver blue be-neath the pale star-light, Coy-ote yap-pin' la-zy on the
2. Noth-in' out there on the plains that you folks need, Noth-in' there that seems to take your

hill,_____ Sleep-y winks of light a-long the far sky-line,
eye._____ Still you got to watch them or they'll all stam-pede,

Time for mill-in' cat-tle to be still._____ So now the light-ning's far a-way; The
Plung-in' down some 'rro-yo bank to die._____

coy-ote's noth-in' skeer-y, just sing-in' to her dear-ie. Yah-ho, a-mol-la hol-i-day, So

set-tle down, ye cat-tle, till the morn-ing.

THE COWBOY

1. All day on the prai - rie in a sad - dle I ride, Not
2. I wash in a pud - dle and ___ wipe on a sack, I

e - ven a dog, boys, to trot by my side. My fire I must
car - ry my ward - robe a - long on my back. My ceil - ing's the

kin - dle with chips gath - ered round, And boil my own cof - fee with -
sky, ___ my car - pet the grass, My mu - sic the low - ing of

out be - ing ground. My bread lack - ing leav - en I bake in a
herds as they pass. My books are the brooks, ___ my ser - mons the

pot, And I sleep on the ground ___ for want of a cot.
stones, My ___ par - son a wolf on a pul - pit of bones.

3. And then if my cooking is not too complete,
   No one can blame me for not wanting to eat.
   But show me a man that can sleep more profound
   Than the cowboy who stretches himself on the ground.
   My books teach me ever consistence to prize,
   My sermons, the small things I shall not despise.

4. My parson remarks from his pulpit of bones
   That the Lord favors those who look out for their own.
   But between me and love there's a gulf very wide,
   And some luckier fellow may call her his bride.
   My friends gently hint I am coming to grief,
   But men must make money and women have beef.

THE COWBOY'S LAMENT

1. As I_____ walked out in the streets of La - re - do, As I_____ walked
2. "I see by your out - fit that you are a cow - boy." These words he did
3. "Oh, beat the drum slow - ly and play the fife low - ly;_____ Play the Dead

out in La - re - do one day, I_____ spied a young cow-boy wrapped up in white
say as I bold - ly stepped by. "Come___ sit down be - side me and hear my sad
March as you car - ry me a - long. Take me to the green val - ley and lay the sod

lin - en, Wrapped up in white lin - en and__ cold as the clay.
sto - ry; I'm shot in the breast and I___ know I must die."
o'er me, For I'm a young cow - boy and I know I've done wrong."

4. "It was once in the saddle
   I used to go dashing;
   It was once in the saddle
   I used to go gay.
   First to the dram house
   and then to the card house,
   Got shot in the breast
   and I'm dying today."

5. "Get six jolly cowboys
   to carry my coffin;
   Get six pretty maidens
   to bear up my pall.
   Put bunches of roses
   all over my coffin,
   Put roses to deaden
   the clods as they fall."

6. "Go bring me a cup,
   a cup of cold water
   To cool my parched lips,"
   the young cowboy said.
   Before I returned,
   the spirit had left him
   And gone to its Maker—
   the cowboy was dead.

7. We beat the drum slowly
   and played the fife lowly,
   And bitterly wept
   as we bore him along.
   For we all loved our comrade,
   so brave, young, and handsome,
   We all loved our comrade
   although he'd done wrong.

LA CUCARACHA

La cu-ca-ra - cha, la cu-ca-ra - cha, ya__ no pue-de cam-i -

nar; por-que no tie - ne,__ por-que le fal - ta__ mar - i-jua-na que fu -

Fine

mar. 1. Cuan - do u - no quier-e_a u - na__ Y_es - ta u - na no lo
2. Ya mur - ió la cu - ca - ra - cha, Ya__ la lle - van a en -
3. Mi ve - ci - na de_a-hí_en - fren - te__ Se__ lla - ma - ba Do - ña

quie - re,__ Es lo mis - mo que si_un cal - vo__ En__ ca-lle_en-cuen-tra un pei-ne.__
te - rrar, En-tre cuat - ro zo - pil - o - tes__ Y_un ra - tón de sa-cris - tán.__
Cla - ra,__ Y si no se_hu-bie - ra muer-to__ Aún as - í se lla-ma - ra.__

4. Un panadero fue a misa,
   No encontrando que rezar,
   Le pidió a la Virgen pura,
   Marihuana pa' fumar.

5. De la patillas de un moro
   tengo que hacer una escoba,
   para que barra el cuartel
   la infantería española.

6. Con las barbas de Carranza
   voy a hacer una toquilla
   pa' ponérsela al sombrero
   de su padre Pancho Villa.

THE DAYS OF '49

1. I'm____ old Tom Moore from the bum-mer's shore in the good old gold-en days. They
2. My____ com-rades, they all____ loved me well,__ a jol-ly sau-cy crew; A
3. There was old Lame Jess, a____ hard old cuss, who ne-ver did re-pent. He

call me a bum-mer and a gin-sot, too, but__ what care I for praise? I
few hard__ cas-es, I____ will ad-mit, though they were brave and true. What-
ne-ver was known to__ miss a drink nor to e-ver spend a cent. But

wan-der a-round from town to town just like a rov-ing sign, And the
ev-er the pinch they ne'er would flinch, they'd nev-er fret or whine; Like__
old Lame Jess, like all__ the rest, to death he did re-sign, And__

peo-ple all say, "There goes Tom Moore of the days of for-ty - nine." In the
good old bricks they stood the kicks in the days of for-ty - nine.
in__ his bloom went up the flume in the days of for-ty - nine.

days of old, in the days of gold, how oft-times I re-pine For the days of old when we

dug up the gold in the days of for-ty - nine.

4. There was Poker Bill, one of the boys,
   who was always in for a game;
   Whether he lost or whether he won,
   to him it was all the same.
   He would ante up and draw his cards,
   he would go a hatful blind.
   In the game of death, Bill lost his breath
   in the days of forty-nine.
   (Chorus)

5. There was New York Jake, the butcher boy,
   he was always getting tight,
   And every time that he'd get full,
   he was spoiling for a fight;
   But Jake rampaged against a knife
   in the hands of old Bob Pine,
   And over Jake they held a wake
   in the days of forty-nine.
   (Chorus)

6. There was Ragshag Bill from Buffalo,
   I never will forget,
   He would roar all day and he'd roar all night
   and I guess he's roaring yet.
   One night he fell in a prospect hole
   in a roaring bad design,
   And in that hole he roared out his soul
   in the days of forty-nine.
   (Chorus)

7. Of all the comrades that I've had
   there's none that's left to boast,
   And I'm left alone in my misery
   like some poor wandering ghost;
   And as I pass from town to town
   they call me the rambling sign,
   "There goes Tom Moore, a bummer
   shore, of the days of forty-nine."
   (Chorus)

DOWN IN THE VALLEY

1. Down in the val - ley, val - ley so low,_____ Hang your head o -
2. Ros - es love sun - shine, vio - lets love dew,_____ An - gels in heav -

ver, hear the wind blow._____ Hear the wind blow, dear,
en, know I love you._____ Know I love you, dear,

hear the wind blow,_____ Hang your head o - ver, hear the wind blow._____
know I love you,_____ An - gels in heav - en know I love you._____

THE DREARY, DREARY LIFE

1. A cow-boy's life is a drear-y, drear-y life, Some
(Chorus) Half - past four, the noise - y cook will roar,

say it's free from care; Round-ing up the cat-tle from
"Whoop-a - whoop - a - hey!" Slow-ly you will rise with

morn-ing till night In the mid-dle of the prair-ie so bare.
sleep-y - feel-ing eyes, The sweet, dream-y night passed a - way.

2. The greener lad
   he thinks it's play,
   He'll soon peter out
   on a cold rainy day,
   With his big bell spurs
   and his Spanish hoss,
   He'll swear to you
   he was once a boss.
   (Chorus)

3. The cowboy's life
   is a dreary, dreary life,
   He's driven through
   the heat and cold;
   While the rich man's a-sleeping
   on his velvet couch,
   Dreaming of his
   silver and gold.
   (Chorus)

4. Spring-time sets in,
   double trouble will begin,
   The weather is so
   fierce and cold;
   Clothes are wet
   and frozen to our necks,
   The cattle we can
   scarcely hold.
   (Chorus)

5. The cowboy's life
   is a dreary one,
   He works all day to the
   setting of the sun;
   And then his day's work
   is not done,
   For there's his night herd
   to go on.
   (Chorus)

6. The wolves and owls
      with their terrifying howls
   Will disturb us in our
      midnight dream,
      As we lie on our slickers
      on a cold, rainy night
   Way over on the
      Pecos stream.
   (Chorus)

7. You are speaking of your farms,
      you are speaking of your charms,
   You are speaking of your
      silver and gold;
   But a cowboy's life
      is a dreary, dreary life,
   He's driven through the
      heat and cold.
   (Chorus)

8. Some folks say that we are
      free from care,
   Free from all
      other harm;
   But we round up the cattle
      from morning till night
   Way over on the
      prairie so dry.
   (Chorus)

9. I used to run about,
      now I stay at home,
   Take care of my
      wife and child;
   Nevermore to roam,
      always stay at home,
   Take care of my
      wife and child.
   (Chorus)

THE DYING RANGER

1. The sun was sink - ing in the west, And fell with lin - g'ring
2. A group had gath - ered round him, His com - rades in the
3. When to stop the life - blood flow - ing He found 'twas all in

ray Through the bran - ches of the for - est, Where a wound - ed ran - ger
fight, A tear rolled down each man - ly cheek As he bid a last good-
vain, The tears rolled down each man's cheek Like light show - ers of

lay; 'Neath the shad of a pal - met - to And the sun - set sil - v'ry
night. One tried and true com - pan - ion Was kneel - ing by his
rain. Up spoke the no - ble ran - ger, "Boys, weep no more for

sky, Far a - way from his home in Tex - as, They laid him down to die.
side, To stop his life-blood flow - ing, But a - las, in vain he tried.
me, I am cros - sing the deep wat - ers To a coun - try that is free.

4. "Draw closer to me, comrades,
   and listen to what I say,
   I am going to tell a story
   While my spirit hastens away.
   Way back in Northwest Texas,
   That good old Lone Star state,
   There is one that for my coming
   With a weary heart will wait.

5. "A fair young girl, my sister,
   My only joy, my pride,
   She was my friend from boyhood,
   I had no one left beside.
   I have loved her as a brother,
   And with a father's care
   I have strove from grief and sorrow
   Her gentle heart to spare.

6. "My mother, she lies sleeping
   Beneath the church-yard sod,
And many a day has passed away
   Since her spirit fled to God.
My father, he lies sleeping
   Beneath the deep blue sea,
I have no other kindred,
   There are none but Nell and me.

7. "But our country was invaded
   And they called for volunteers;
She threw her arms around me,
   Then burst into tears,
Saying, 'Go, my darling brother,
   Drive those traitors from our shore,
My heart may need your presence,
   But our country needs you more.'

8. "It is true I love my country,
   For her I gave my all.
If it hadn't been for. my sister,
   I would be content to fall.
I am dying, comrades, dying,
   She will never see me more,
But in vain she'll wait my coming
   By our little cabin door.

9. "Comrades, gather closer
   And listen to my dying prayer.
Who will be to her as a brother,
   And shield her with a brother's care?"
Up spake the noble rangers,
   They answered one and all,
"We will be to her as brothers
   Till the last one does fall."

10. One glad smile of pleasure
   O'er the ranger's face was spread;
One dark, convulsive shadow,
   And the ranger boy was dead.
Far from his darling sister
   We laid him down to rest
With his saddle for a pillow
   And his gun across his breast.

GIT ALONG, LITTLE DOGIES

1. As I was a-walk-ing one morn-ing for plea-sure, I spied a cow-punch-er a-
2. It's ear-ly in spring that we round up the do-gies, We mark them and brand them and

rid-in' a-long. His hat was throwed back and his spurs were a-jing-lin', And
bob off their tails. We round up our hor-ses, load up the chuck wa-gon, And

as he ap-proached he was sing-in' this song: Whoop-ee ti-yi-yo,— git a-
then throw the do-gies out on-to the trail.

long lit-tle do-gies, It's your mis-for-tune and none of my own. Whoop-ee ti-yi yo,— git a-

long lit-tle do-gies, You know that Wy-o-ming will be your new home

3. It's whooping and yelling and drivin' the dogies
   And oh how I wish you would only go on!
   It's whooping and punching, go on, little dogies,
   You know that Wyoming will be your new home. *(Chorus)*

4. Some boys, they go up on the trail just for pleasure,
   But that's where they get it most awfully wrong.
   You haven't a notion the trouble they give us,
   It takes all our time to keep moving along. *(Chorus)*

5. Your mother was raised way down in Texas,
   Where the jimson weed and the sandburs grow.
   We'll fill you up on prickly pear and cholla,
   Then throw you on the trail to Idaho. *(Chorus)*

GOODBYE, OLD PAINT

Good - bye, Old Paint, I'm a - leav - in' Chey - enne. Good - bye, Old Paint, I'm a - leav - in' Chey -

enne.
1. My foot's in the stir - rup, my po - ny won't___ stan', I'm a - leav - in' Chey -
2. Old Paint's a good po - ny, he pac - es when he can,___ Good - bye,___ Old
3. Go hitch up your hor - ses and feed 'em some___ hay,___ An' set your - self by

enne, an' I'm off to Mon - tan'. Good - bye Old Paint, I'm a - leav - in' Chey - enne. Good -
Paint,___ I'm off to Mon - tan'.
me___ as long as you'll stay.

bye, Old Paint, I'm a - leav - in' Chey - enne.

4. My horses ain't hungry, they won't eat your hay;
   My wagon is loaded and rollin' away.
   (Chorus)

5. My foot's in the stirrup, my bridle's in hand,
   Goodbye, Old Paint, my horses won't stand.
   (Chorus)

32

HO! WESTWARD HO!

1. "The star of em - pire," po - ets say, Ho! West-ward Ho! "For - ev - er takes its
2. Our Pil - grim Fa - thers sang the song, Ho! West-ward Ho! Here right should tri - umph

on - ward way!" Ho! West-ward Ho! That this be pro - ven in our land,
o - ver wrong! Ho! West-ward Ho! Still west - ward man - y thou-sands flock,

Ho! West - ward Ho! It seems Je - ho - vah's great com - mand. Ho! West-ward Ho!
Ho! West - ward Ho! And sing the shout from Ply - mouth Rock, Ho! West-ward Ho!

Ho! West - ward! Soon the world shall know That

all is grand in the west - ern land; Ho! West - ward Ho!

3. 'Tis ever thus, the people cry, Ho! Westward Ho!
   And from the eastern cities fly, Ho! Westward Ho!
   To live on God's most glorious land, Ho! Westward Ho!
   Where hearts and thougts are ever grand, Ho! Westward Ho! (*Chorus*)

4. The western fields give thousands wealth, Ho! Westward Ho!
   And yield to all a glowing health, Ho! Westward Ho!
   For all inclined to honest toil, Ho! Westward Ho!
   Secure their fortunes from the soil, Ho! Westward Ho! (*Chorus*)

5. We love the glorious western land, Ho! Westward Ho!
   For here the people's hearts expand, Ho! Westward Ho!
   And on the prairies broad and grand, Ho! Westward Ho!
   We all can see Jehovah's hand, Ho! Westward Ho! (*Chorus*)

HOME ON THE RANGE

1. Oh, give me a home where the buf-fa-lo roam, Where the deer and the an-te-lope
2. How of-ten at night when the heav-ens are bright With the light from the glit-ter-ing

play,_____ Where_ sel-dom is heard a dis-cour-ag-ing word And the skies are not
stars,_____ Have I stood here a-mazed and_ asked as I gazed If their glo-ry ex-

clou-dy all day._____ Home, home on the range,_____ Where the deer and the
ceeds that of ours._____

an-te-lope play._____ Where sel-dom is heard a dis-cour-ag-ing

word, And the skies are not clou-dy all day.

3. Where the air is so pure, the zephyrs so free,
   The breezes so balmy and light.
   That I would not exchange my home on the range
   For all the cities so bright.
   (*Chorus*)

4. Oh, I love those wild flow'rs in this dear land of ours,
   The curlew I love to hear scream.
   And I love the white rocks and the antelope flocks
   That graze on the mountaintops green.
   (*Chorus*)

I RIDE AN OLD PAINT

1. I ride an old Paint, I_____ lead an old_____ Dan. I'm__ off to Mon-
2. ... Old___ Bill Jones had two daugh-ters and a song:_____ One went to
3. Oh, when__ I die,___ take my sad-dle from the wall, Put it on_____ my

tan'____ for to throw the hoo-li-han. They feed in the cou-lees, they
Den-ver, and the oth-er went__ wrong. His__ wife,___ she died in a
po-ny and__ lead him from the stall. Tie my bones to his back, turn our

wa-ter in the draw; Their___ tails are all mat-ted, their backs are all
pool-room__ fight, And he sings__ this song__ from morn-ing till
fac-es to the west, And we'll ride___ the prai-ries we love____ the

raw. Ride a-round, lit-tle do-gies, ride a-round___ them slow, For the
night:_____
best._____

fi - ery and snuf-fy are a-rar-in' to go.

JACK O' DIAMONDS

1. Oh, Mol - ly, oh, Mol - ly, 'tis for your___ sake a - lone That I leave my old
2. My foot's in my stir - rup, my___ bri - dle's in my hand. I'm___ goin' to leave
3. They say I drink whis - key, but my mon - ey is my own, And___ them that don't

par - ents, my house___ and my home, That I leave my old par - ents, you caused me to
Mol - ly, the fair - est in the land. Her___ par - ents don't like me, they say I'm too
like me can leave___ me a - lone. I'll___ eat when I'm hun - gry, I'll drink when I'm

roam. I'm an old reb - el sol - dier and Dix - ie's my home. Jack o'
poor, They___ say I'm un - worth - y to en - ter her door.
dry, And___ when I get thir - sty I'll lay down and cry.

Dia - monds, Jack o' Dia - monds, I know you of old; You've robbed my poor pock - ets of

sil - ver and gold. Oh,___ whis - key, you vil - lian, you've been my down - fall; You've

kicked me, you've cuffed me, but I love you for all.

4. I will build me a big castle
   on yonder mountain high,
   Where my true love can see me
   when she comes riding by,
   Where my true love can see me
   and help me to mourn,
   I am a rabble soldier
   and Dixie is my home.
   (Chorus)

5. I'll get up in my saddle,
   my quirt I'll take in hand;
   I'll think of you, Mollie,
   when in some far distant land;
   I'll think of you, Molly,
   you caused me to roam,
   I am a rabble soldier
   and Dixie is my home.
   (Chorus)

6. I've rambled and trambled
   this wide world around,
   But it's for the rabble army,
   dear Molly, I'm bound,
   It is to the rabble army,
   dear Molly, I roam,
   I am a rabble soldier
   and Dixie is my home.
   (Chorus)

7. I have rambled and gambled
   all my money away,
   But it's with the rabble army,
   O Molly, I must stay,
   It is with the rabble army,
   O Molly I must roam,
   I am a rabble soldier
   and Dixie is my home.
   (Chorus)

JESSE JAMES

3. It was Robert Ford, the dirty little coward,
   And I wonder how he feels,
   For he slept in Jesse's bed and he ate o' Jesse's bread,
   But he laid Jesse James in his grave.

4. It was with his brother Frank that he robbed the Gallatin Bank,
   An' carried the money from the town;
   It was at that very place that they had a little chase,
   For they shot ol' Captain Sheets to the ground.

5. They went to a crossing, not very far from there,
   And there they did the same,
   For the agent on his knees delivered up the keys
   To the outlaws, Frank an' Jesse James.

6. It was on a Wednesday night, not a star was in sight,
   When they robbed the Glendale train.
   Those people, they did say, for many miles away,
   It was robbed by Frank an' Jesse James.

7. Then on a Saturday night, Jesse was at home,
   Just talking with his family brave,
   When Robert Ford came along like a thief in the night,
   And laid poor Jesse in his grave.

8. Now, the people held their breath when they heard of Jesse's death.
   They wondered how he came to die.
   It was one of his own gang called little Robert Ford,
   An' he shot Jesse James on the sly.

9. Jesse went to his rest with his hand upon his breast.
   And there are many who never saw his face.
   He was born one day in the County of Clay,
   And he came from a solitary race.

10. This song was made by Billy Gashade
    As soon as the news did arrive.
    He said there's no one man with the law in his hand
    Could ever take ol' Jesse James alive.

11. Oh, they laid poor Jesse in his grave, yes, Lord;
    They laid Jesse James in his grave.
    Oh, he took from the rich and he gave to the poor,
    But, they laid Jesse James in his grave.

LITTLE JOE, THE WRANGLER

1. Lit - tle Joe, the wrang - gler___ He'll wran - gle nev - er
2. It was late___ in the eve - ning___ he rode up to our

more, His___ days with the *re - mu - da* they are o'er;
herd; On a lit - tle Tex-as Po - ny he called Chaw;

T'was a year a - go last A - pril___ he rode in - to our
With his bro - gan shoes and o-ver-alls,___ a tough - er look - in'

herd; Just a lit - tle Tex - as stray, and all a - lone.
kid You___ ne-ver in your life be - fore had saw.

3. His saddle was a Texas "kak,"
   built many years ago,
With an O. K. spur on
   one foot lightly swung;
His "hot roll" in a cotton sack
   so loosely tied behind,
And his canteen from his
   saddle-horn was swung.

4. He said that he had to leave his home,
   his pa had married twice;
And his new ma whipped him
   every day or two;
So he saddled up old Chaw one night
   and lit a shuck this way,
And he's now trying to
   paddle his own canoe.

5. He said if we would give him work,
   he'd do the best he could,
Though he didn't know
   straight up about a cow;
So the boss he cut him out a mount
   and kindly put him on,
For he sorta liked this
   little kid somehow.

6. Learned him to wrangle horses
   and to try to know them all,
And get them in at
   daylight if he could;
To follow the chuck-wagon
   and always hitch the team,
And to help the *cocinero*
   rustle wood.

7. We had driven to the Pecos,
    the weather being fine;
We had camped on the
    south side in a bend;
When a norther commenced blowin',
    we had doubled up our guard,
For it taken all of us
    to hold them in.

8 Little Joe, the wrangler,
    was called out with the rest;
Though the kid had
    scarcely reached the herd,
When the cattle they stampeded,
    like a hailstorm long they fled,
Then we were all
    a-ridin' for the lead.

9. 'Midst the streaks of lightnin'
    a horse we could see in the lead,
'Twas Little Joe,
    the wrangler, in the lead;
He was riding Old Blue Rocket
    with a slicker o'er his head,
A tryin' to check
    the cattle in their speed.

10. At last we got them milling
    and kinda quieted down,
And the extra guard back
    to the wagon went;
But there was one a-missin'
    and we knew it at a glance,
'Twas our little Texas stray,
    poor Wrangling Joe.

11. The next morning just at day break,
    we found where Rocket fell,
Down in a washout
    twenty feet below;
And beneath the horse, mashed to a pulp,
    his spur had rung the knell,
Was our little Texas stray,
    poor Wrangling Joe.

LO QUE DIGO

THE LOVER'S LAMENT

LAS MAÑANITAS

1. Es - tas son las ma - ña - ni - tas que can - ta - ba el rey Da - vid a las
2. Si el ser - e - no de la es - qui - na, me qui - sie - ra ha-cer fa - vor. de a - pa -
3. Aho - ra si, se - ñor ser - e - no, le a-grad - ez - co su fa - vor. en - cien -
4. A - ma - po - li - ta do - ra - da de los lla - nos de Te - pic. si no es -

much - a - chas bon - i - tas, Se las cant - a - mos a - quí. Des -
gar su lin - ter - ni - ta mien - tras que pa - sa mi a - mor.
da su lin - ter - ni - ta que ya ha pa - sa - do mi a - mor.
tas en - a - mor - a - da, en - a - mór - a - te de mi.

pier - ta, mi bien, des - pier - ta, mi - ra que ya am-an - e - ció, ya los

pa - jar - i - llos can - tan, La lu - na ya se me - tió.

MY LOVE IS A RIDER

1. My love is a rid - er; wild bron - cos he breaks, But he's
2. The first time I saw him 'twas ear - ly one spring, He was
3. The next time I saw him 'twas late in the fall, He was

pro - mised to quit it, and just for my sake. He
rid - ing a bron - co, a high - head - ed thing. He
swing - ing the la - dies at Tom - lin - son's hall. We

ties up one foot, and the sad - dle puts on; With a
tipped me a wink as he gail - y did go, For he
laughed and we talked as we danced to and fro, Prom-ised

swing and a jump, he is mount - ed and gone.
wished me to look at his buck - ing bron - co.
ne - ver to ride on an - o - ther bron - co.

4. He made me some presents, among them a ring.
   But that which I gave him was a far better thing.
   'Twas a young maiden's heart, and I want you to know
   He won it while riding his bucking bronco.

5. Come all you young maidens, where'er you reside,
   Beware of the cowboy who swings the rawhide.
   He'll court you, and pet you, and leave you, and go
   Up the trail in the spring on his bucking bronco.

NIGHT-HERDING SONG

1. Oh, slow up, do-gies; quit rov-ing a round. You've wan-dered and tram-pled all
2. I've circle herd-ed, trail-herd-ed cross-herd-ed too; But to keep you to-geth-er, that's

o - ver the ground. Oh, graze a-long, do-gies, and feed kind of slow, And don't be for-
what I can't do. My horse is leg - wea-ry, and I'm aw-ful tired, But if I let you

ev - er on the go._____ Move slow lit-tle do - gies, move slow._____
get a-way, I'm sure to get fired. Bunch up, lit-tle do - gies, bunch up._____

3. Oh, say, little dogies, when you goin' to lay down
   And quit this forever sifting around?
   My limbs are weary, my seat is sore;
   Oh, lay down, dogies, like you've laid down before.
   Lay down, little dogies, lay down.

4. Oh, lay still, dogies, since you have laid down.
   Stretch away out on the big open ground.
   Snore loud, little dogies, and drown the wild sound;
   They'll all go away when the day rolls around.
   Lay still, little dogies, lay still.

THE OLD CHISHOLM TRAIL

1. Well, __ come a-long, boys, and __ lis-ten to my tale; __ I'll tell you of my trou-bles on the
2. With a ten - dol-lar horse and a for - ty - dol-lar sad-dle, I start-ted in __ herd-ing these

old Chis-holm Trail. Come a ti yi yip-py, yip-py yay, yip-py yay Come a ti yi yip-py, yip-py yay. __
Tex-as __ cat-tle. __

3. I'm up in the morning before daylight;
   Before I sleep the moon shines bright. *(Chorus)*

4. Oh, it's bacon and beans most every day;
   We'll soon be eating this prairie hay. *(Chorus)*

5. With my seat in the saddle and my hand on the horn,
   I'm the best cowpuncher that ever was born. *(Chorus)*

6. No chaps, no slicker, and it's pourin' down rain;
   I swear I'll never night-herd again. *(Chorus)*

7. A stray in the herd and the boss said, "Kill it!"
   So I shot it in the rump with the handle of a skillet. *(Chorus)*

8. I went to the boss to draw my roll,
   And he had me figured out nine dollars in the hole. *(Chorus)*

9. Me and my boss we had a little spat,
   So I hit him in the face with my ten-gallon hat. *(Chorus)*

10. I'm going to sell my horse, going to sell my saddle,
    'Cause I'm tired of punching these Longhorn cattle. *(Chorus)*

11. With my knees in the saddle and my seat in the sky,
    I'll quit punchin' cows in the sweet by-and-by. *(Chorus)*

48

OLD DAN TUCKER

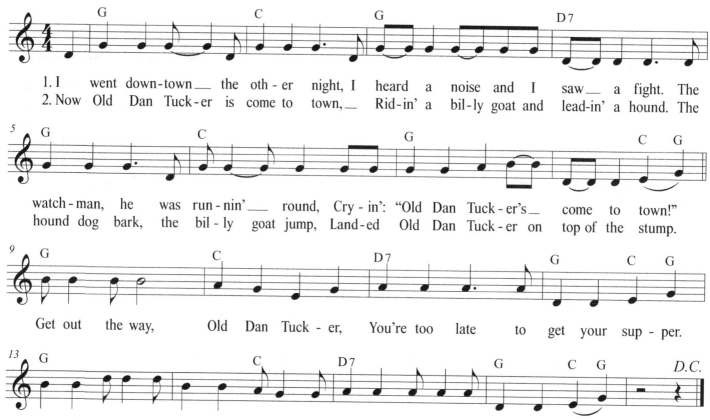

1. I went down-town___ the oth-er night, I heard a noise and I saw___ a fight. The
2. Now Old Dan Tuck-er is come to town,___ Rid-in' a bil-ly goat and lead-in' a hound. The

watch-man, he was run-nin'___ round, Cry-in': "Old Dan Tuck-er's___ come to town!"
hound dog bark, the bil-ly goat jump, Land-ed Old Dan Tuck-er on top of the stump.

Get out the way, Old Dan Tuck-er, You're too late to get your sup-per.

Sup-per's o-ver and break-fast cook-in', But Old Dan Tuck-er just stand there look-in'.

3. Old Dan Tucker went down to the mill
To get some meal to put in the swill.
The miller swore by the point of his knife
That he never seen such a man in his life.

4. Old Dan Tucker, he got drunk,
Fell in the fire and kicked up a chunk.
A red-hot coal rolled in his shoe,
And oh my gosh how the ashes flew!

5. Old Dan Tucker was a fine old man,
Washed his face in a frying pan.
Combed his hair with a wagon wheel,
Died with a toothache in his heel.

6. Now Old Dan Tucker is come to town
Swingin' the ladies round and round.
First to the right and then to the left.
Then the girl that he loves best.

7. Old Dan and me, we did fall out,
And what do you think it was about?
He stepped on my corn. I kicked his shin,
And that's the way it all begin.

OLD TEXAS

POOR LONESOME COWBOY

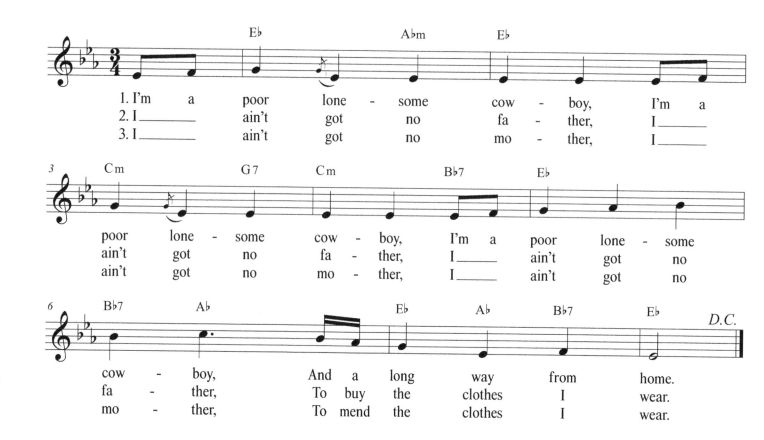

1. I'm a poor lone - some cow - boy, I'm a
2. I_____ ain't got no fa - ther, I_____
3. I_____ ain't got no mo - ther, I_____

poor lone - some cow - boy, I'm a poor lone - some
ain't got no fa - ther, I_____ ain't got no
ain't got no mo - ther, I_____ ain't got no

cow - boy, And a long way from home.
fa - ther, To buy the clothes I wear.
mo - ther, To mend the clothes I wear.

4. I ain't got no sister,
   I ain't got no sister,
   I ain't got no sister,
   To go and play with me.

5. I ain't got no brother,
   I ain't got no brother,
   I ain't got no brother,
   To drive the steers with me.

6 I ain't got no sweetheart,
  I ain't got no sweetheart,
  I ain't got no sweetheart,
  To sit and talk with me.

THE RAILROAD CORRAL

1. We're up in the morn-ing at break-ing of day; The chuck wag-on's bus-y, the
2. Come take up your cinch-es and shake out your reins, Come wake your old bron-co and
3. The sun cir-cles up-ward, the steers as they plod Are pound-ing to pow-der the
4. But tie up your ker-chief and ply up your nag, Come dry up your grum-bles and

flap-jacks in play. The ___ herd is a-stir o-ver hill-side and vale With the
break for the plains. Come ___ roust out your steers from the long chap-ar-ral, For the
hot prair-ie sod. And it seems, as the dust makes you diz-zy and sick, That we'll
try not to lag. Come drive out your steers from the long chap-ar-ral, For we're

night rid-ers crowd-ing them on-to the trail.
out-fit is off to the rail-road cor-ral.
ne-ver reach noon and the cool shad-y creek.
far on the road to the rail-road cor-ral.

5. The afternoon shadows
   are starting to lean,
   When the chuck wagon sticks
   in a marshy ravine.
   The herd scatters farther
   than vision can look.
   You can bet all the punchers
   will help out the cook.

6. Come shake out your rawhide
   and shake it up fair,
   Come break your old bronco
   and take in your share.
   Come roust out your steers
   from the long chaparral,
   For it's all in the drive
   to the railroad corral.

7. But the longest of days
   must reach evening at last,
   The hills are all climbed
   and the creeks are all passed.
   The tired herd droops
   in the yellowing light;
   Let 'em loaf if they will,
   for the railroad's in sight.

8. So flap up your holster
   and snap up your belt,
   And strap up your saddle
   whose lap you have felt.
   Goodbye to the steers
   from the long chaparral,
   There's a town that's a trump
   by the railroad corral.

RED RIVER VALLEY

1. From this val - ley they say you are leav - ing,_____ We will miss your bright
Chorus: Come and sit by my side O my dar - ling,_____ Do not hast - en to

eyes and sweet smile._____ For they say you are tak - ing the sun - shine____
bid me a - dieu._____ But re - mem - ber the Red Riv - er Val - ley,____

— That____ bright - ens our path - way a - while._____
— And the girl that has loved you so true._____

2. For a long time I have been waiting
   For those dear words you never would say,
   But at last all my fond hopes have vanished,
   For they say you are going away.
   (*Chorus*)

3. Won't you think of the valley you're leaving?
   Oh how lonely, how sad it will be.
   Oh think of the fond heart you're breaking,
   And the grief you are causing me to see?
   (*Chorus*)

4. From this valley they say you are going;
   When you go, may your darling go too?
   Would you leave her behind unprotected
   When she loves no other but you?
   (*Chorus*)

5. I have promised you, darling, that never
   Will a word from my lips cause you pain;
   And my life, it will be yours forever
   If you only will love me again.
   (*Chorus*)

6. Must the past with its joys be blighted
   By the future of sorrow and pain,
   And the vows that was spoken be slighted?
   Don't you think you can love me again?
   (*Chorus*)

7. As you go to your home by the ocean,
   May you never forget those sweet hours,
   That we spent in Red River Valley,
   And the love we exchanged 'mid the flowers.
   (*Chorus*)

8. There never could be such a longing
   In the heart of a pure maiden's breast,
   That dwells in the heart you are breaking
   As I wait in my home in the West.
   (*Chorus*)

9. And the dark maiden's prayer for her lover
   To the Spirit that rules over the world;
   May his pathway be ever in sunshine,
   Is the prayer of the Red River girl.
   (*Chorus*)

SAM BASS

1. Sam Bass was born in In - di - a - na, __ it was his na - tive home, And __ at the age of sev - en - teen young Sam be - gan to roam. Sam first came out to Tex - as __ a cow - boy for to be, __ A __ kind - er - heart - ed fel - low __ you sel - dom ev - er see. __

2. Sam used to deal __ in race stock, one called the Den - ton mare. __ He __ matched her in scrub rac - es and took her to the fair. __ Sam used to coin the mon - ey __ and spent it just as free; __ He __ al - ways drank good whis - key __ where - ev - er he might be. __

3. Sam left the Col - lins' ranch __ in __ the mer - ry month of May, __ With a herd of Tex - as cat - tle the Black __ Hills to see. __ Sold out at Cus - ter Ci - ty __ and then got on a spree, And a tough - er set of cow - boys you sel - dom ev - er see. __

4. On their way back to Texas they robbed the U.P. train;
   And then split up in couples and started out again.
   Joe Collins and his partner were overtaken soon,
   With all their hard-earned money they had to meet their doom.

5. Sam made it back to Texas all right side up with care,
   Rode into the town of Denton with all his friends to share.
   Sam's life was short in Texas, three robberies he did do,
   He robbed all the passenger, mail, and express cars too.

6. Sam had four companions, four bold and daring lads,
   They were Richardson, Jackson, Joe Collins, and Old Dad;
   Four more bold and daring cowboys the rangers never knew,
   They whipped the Texas rangers and ran the Boys in Blue.

7. Sam had another companion, called Arkansas for short,
   Was shot by a Texas ranger by the name of Thomas Floyd;
   O, Tom is a big six-footer and thinks he's mighty fly,
   But I can tell you his racket, he's a deadbeat on the sly.

8. Jim Murphy was arrested, and then released on bail,
   He jumped his bond at Tyler and then took the train for Terrell;
   But Mayor Jones had posted Jim and that was all a stall,
   'Twas only a plan to capture Sam before the coming of fall.

9. Sam met his fate at Round Rock, July the twenty-first,
   They pierced poor Sam with rifle balls and emptied out his purse.
   Poor Sarn he is a corpse and six foot under clay,
   And Jackson's in the bushes trying to get away.

10. Jim had borrowed Sam's good gold and didn't want to pay,
    The only shot he saw was to give poor Sam away.
    He sold out Sam and Barnes and left their friends to mourn,
    O what a scorching Jim will get when Gabriel blows his horn.

11. And so he sold out Sam and Barnes and left their friends to mourn,
    What a scorching Jim will get when Gabriel blows his horn.
    Perhaps he's got to heaven, there's none of us can say,
    But if I'm right in my surmise he's gone the other way.

SWEET BETSY FROM PIKE

1. Oh don't you rem - em - ber sweet Bet - sy from Pike, Who crossed the big
2. One eve - ning quite ear - ly, they camped on the Platte, 'Twas near by the
3. They soon reached the de - sert, where Bet - sy gave out, And down in the

moun - tains with her lov - er Ike, With two yoke of cat - tle, a
road on a green sha - dy flat; Where Bet - sy, quite ti - red, laid
sand she lay rol - ling a - bout; While Ike in great tears____ looked

large yel - low dog, A_____ tall Shang-hai roos - ter, and one spot - ted hog; Say-ing
down to re - pose, While with won - der Ike gazed on his Pike Coun - ty Rose
on in sur - prise, Say - ing, "Bet - sy get up, you'll get sand in your eyes."

good - bye, Pike Coun - ty, Fare - well for a while; We'll____

come back a - gain When we've panned out our pile.

4. Sweet Betsy got up in a great deal of pain,
   And declared she'd go back to Pike County again.
   Then Ike heaved a sigh and they fondly embraced,
   And she traveled along with his arm 'round her waist.
   (Chorus)

5. The Shanghai ran off and the cattle all died,
   The last piece of bacon that morning was fried;
   Poor Ike got discouraged, and Betsy got mad,
   The dog wagged his tail and looked wonderfully sad.
   (Chorus)

6. One morning they climbed up a very high hill,
   And with wonder looked down into old Placerville;
   Ike shouted and said, as he cast his eyes down,
   "Sweet Betsy, my darling, we've got to Hangtown."
   (Chorus)

7. Long Ike and Sweet Betsy attended a dance,
   Where Ike wore a pair of his Pike County pants,
   Sweet Betsy was covered with ribbons and rings.
   Quoth Ike, "You're an angel, but where are your wings?"
   (Chorus)

8. A miner said "Betsy, will you dance with me?"
   "I will, old hoss, if you don't make too free;
   But don't dance me hard. Do you want to know why?
   Dog on ye, I'm chock full of strong alkali."
   (Chorus)

9. Long Ike and Sweet Betsy got married, of course,
   But Ike getting jealous obtained a divorce;
   And Betsy, well satisfied, said with a shout,
   "Goodbye, you big lummux, I'm glad you backed out,"

Last Chorus:
   Saying goodbye, dear Isaac,
   Farewell for a while.
   But come back in time
   To replenish my pile.

58

THE TENDERFOOT

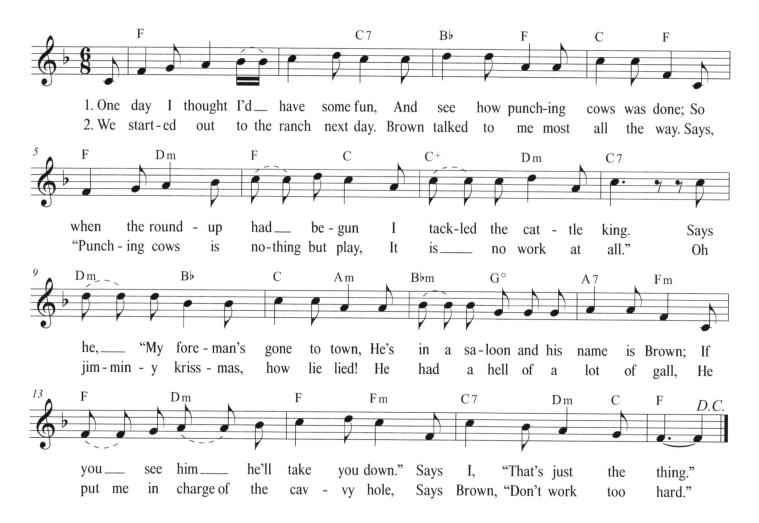

1. One day I thought I'd have some fun, And see how punch-ing cows was done; So
2. We start-ed out to the ranch next day. Brown talked to me most all the way. Says,

when the round-up had be-gun I tack-led the cat-tle king. Says
"Punch-ing cows is no-thing but play, It is no work at all." Oh

he, "My fore-man's gone to town, He's in a sa-loon and his name is Brown; If
jim-min-y kriss-mas, how lie lied! He had a hell of a lot of gall, He

you see him he'll take you down." Says I, "That's just the thing."
put me in charge of the cav-vy hole, Says Brown, "Don't work too hard."

3. Sometimes those cattle would make a break
And across the prairie they would take,
Just like they was running for a stake.
To them it was nothing but play.
Sometimes they would stumble and fall,
Sometimes you couldn't head 'em at all,
And we'd shoot on like a cannonball
Till the ground came in our way.

4. They saddled me up an old gray hack
With a great big seat fast on his back.
They padded him down with gunny sack
And with my bedding too.
When I got on him he left the ground,
Went up in the air and circled around
And when I came down I busted the ground.
I got a terrible fall.

5. They picked me up and carried me in
   And rubbed me down with a picket pin.
   Says, "That's the way they all begin."
   "You're doing fine," says Brown.
   "To-morrow morning if you don't die
   I'll give you another hoss to try."
   Says I, "Oh can't I walk?"
   Says Brown, "Yep, back to town."

6. I've travelled up, I've travelled down,
   I've travelled this wide world all around,
   I've lived in city, I've lived in town;
   I've got this much to say:
   Before you go to punching cows,
   Go kiss your wife, get a heavy insurance upon your life,
   And shoot yourself with a butcher knife,
   For that is the easiest way.

TENTING ON THE OLD CAMPGROUND

THE TEXAS RANGERS

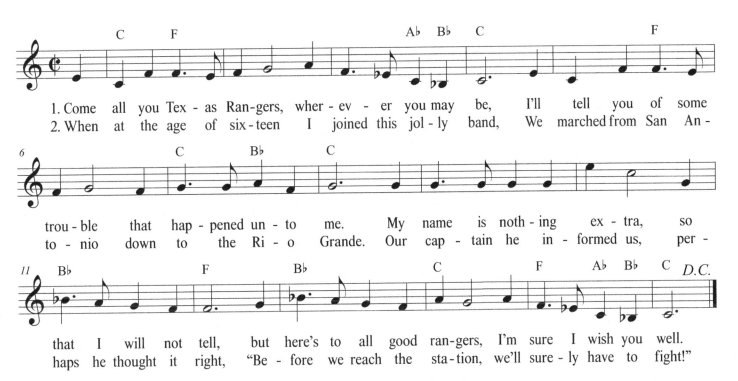

1. Come all you Tex - as Ran-gers, wher - ev - er you may be, I'll tell you of some
2. When at the age of six-teen I joined this jol - ly band, We marched from San An -

trou - ble that hap - pened un - to me. My name is noth - ing ex - tra, so
to - nio down to the Ri - o Grande. Our cap - tain he in - formed us, per -

that I will not tell, but here's to all good ran-gers, I'm sure I wish you well.
haps he thought it right, "Be - fore we reach the sta-tion, we'll sure - ly have to fight!"

3. I saw the smoke ascending, it seemed to hit the sky.
The first thought then came to me, "My times has come to die!"
And when the bugles sounded, our captain gave command,
"To arms, to arms," he shouted, "and by your horses stand."

4. I saw the Indians coming, I heard their awful yell.
My feelings at the moment, no human tongue can tell.
I saw their glittering lances, their arrows around me flew,
Till all my strength had left me, and all my courage too.

5. We fought for five full hours before the strife was o'er.
The likes of dead and wounded, I've never seen before.
And when the sun had risen, the Indians they had fled.
We loaded up our rifles and counted up our dead.

6. Now all of us were wounded, our noble captain slain.
And when the sun was shining across the bloody plain,
Six of the noblest rangers that ever roamed the West,
Were buried by their comrades with arrows in their breasts.

7. Perhaps you have a mother, likewise a sister too.
Perhaps you have a sweetheart, to weep and mourn for you.
If this be your position, although you'd like to roam,
I'll tell you from experience, you'd better stay at home.

EL TORO MORO

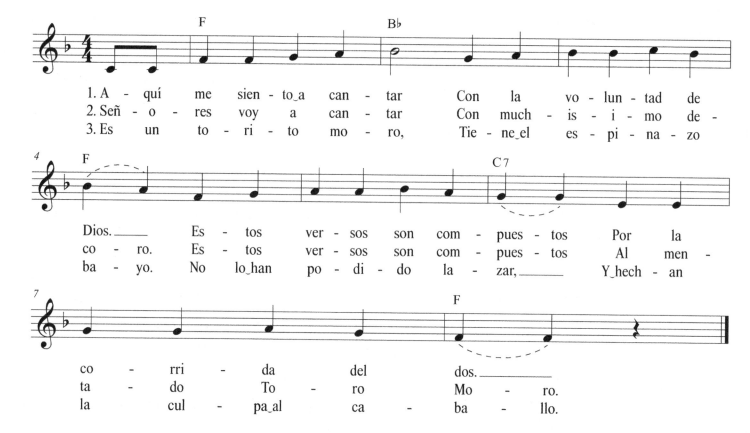

1. A - quí me sien - to_a can - tar Con la vo - lun - tad de
2. Señ - o - res voy a can - tar Con much - is - i - mo de -
3. Es un to - ri - to mo - ro, Tie - ne_el es - pi - na - zo

Dios.____ Es - tos ver - sos son com - pues - tos Por la
co - ro. Es - tos ver - sos son com - pues - tos Al men -
ba - yo. No lo_han po - di - do la - zar,____ Y_hech - an

co - rri - da del dos.____
ta - do To - ro Mo - ro.
la cul - pa_al ca - ba - llo.

4. Buenos pollos lo han corrido,
   Queriendose aprovechar,
   Pero en eso no han podido
   Porque les entra al barral.

5. De becerro lo conocen.
   Desde que tenia tres años
   Ahí anda en la Marcelina,
   Completando los siete años.

6. Se lo halló Euvence García,
   Se lo enseño a su compadre;
   Se pusieron a pensar
   Y se les hizo muy tarde.

7. Y le decía su compadre
   Con un cariño a lo bueno,
   "Lo hecharemos por la brecha
   Y por ahí esta Eugenio."

8. Eugenio como un territo,
   Ya estaba en su agostadero,
   Y al oír el primer grito
   Fué y se hizo al corredero.

9. Cuando Eugenio lo vido
   Al brincar la nopalera,
   Desde ahí se lo fué entrando
   Con su yegua tesonera.

10. El toro se le fué
    En el punto de Placetitas,
    Fué y les dijo a los demás
    Que le truenan las pesuñitas.

11. Decía Manuel Rosas
    En su caballo Cupido,
    "Ojalá que se topara
    Este torito conmigo."

12. Otro día se lo topó
    En ese Plan del Jardín.
    El toro, al brincar la brecha,
    Ahí le pintó un violín.

13. Manuel Rosas lo corrió,
    Diciendo, "Ora si lo laso."
    Pero jamás le tocó
    El polvo del espinazo.

14. Manuel Rosas lo corrió
    Por todo el Plan del Jardín;
    El caballo se voltió,
    Y no lo pudo seguir.

15. Manuel se arrendó a la brecha
    Y topo con su tocayo.
    "Se me fué por hay ansina
    Porque se voltió el caballo."

16. Decía Manuel la Changa,
    Que era un hombre de valor,
    "Héchenmelo por aquí
    Para hacerles un favor."

17. Por toditia la brecha
    Se veia una polvadera;
    Era la Changa diciendo,
    "Yo ya perdí esta carrera."

18. Más allá iba Chon Cortinas,
    Coniendo y moviendo un brazo,
    "Ese toro tiene espinas;
    Por eso yo no lo laso."

19. Dijo Macario Mayorgua,
    Viéndolo tan apurado,
    "Voy a ver a mi compadre
    Ya tendrá el rodeo dado."

20. Cuando Euvence lo vido
    Ya venía muy ajilado,
    Con sonrisas nos decía,
    "El torito está amarrado."

21. Decía Eugenio Cantú
    En la orilla de un mogote,
    "Héchenmelo por aquí
    Pa doblarle un calabrote."

22. Eugenio se lo lasó
    Por no verlos batallar,
    Fué y les dijo a los demás
    Que lo fueran a llevar.

23. Decía Euvence Carcía
    En el tordillo grandote,
    "Mancuémenmelo con los bueyes,
    Llévenlo pa'l Tecolote."

24. Por todo lo de la brecha
    El fuego está cerrado.
    Le dijeron al patrón
    Que el toro estaba amarrado.

25. Lo llevamos para Norias;
    Lo embarcamos pa' For Wes.
    Ya se fué el Torito Moro;
    Ya no volverá otra vez.

26. Y con esta me despido
    Y sin dilación ninguna.
    El que compuso estos versos
    Se llama Miguel de la Luna.

THE TRAIL TO MEXICO

1. It was in the ___ mer - ry ___ month of May
2. It was when I em - braced her in my arms,

When I start - ed for
I ___ thought ___ she

Tex - as far a - way,
had ten thou-sand charms;

I ___ left ___ my dar - ling girl ___ be -
Her car - es - ses were soft, her kis-ses were

hind;
sweet,

She said her ___ heart
Say - ing, "We'll get mar -

was ___ on - ly mine.
ried next time we meet."

3. It was in the year of 'eighty-three
   That A. J. Stinson hired me;
   He says, "Young man, I want you to go
   And follow this herd into Mexico."

4. Well, it was early in the year
   When I started out to drive those steers;
   Through sleet and snow 'twas a lonesome go
   As the herd rolled on into Mexico.

5. When I arrived in Mexico
   I wanted to see my girl but I could not go;
   So I wrote a letter to my dear
   But not a word for years did I hear.

6. Well, I started back to my once loved home,
   Inquired for the girl I had called my own;
   They said she had married a richer life,
   Therefore, wild cowboy, seek another wife.

7. "O buddy, O buddy, please stay at home,
   Don't forever be on the roam.
   There is many a girl more true than I,
   So pray don't go where the bullets fly."

8. "O curse your gold and your silver too.
   God pity a girl that won't prove true.
   I'll travel west where the bullets fly.
   I'll stay on the trail till the day I die."

THE WABASH CANNONBALL

1. From the great At - lan - tic O - cean to the wide Pa - ci - fic shore, From the
2. Well, ___ lis - ten to the jin - gle, the ___ rum - ble, and the roar, As she

queen of flow - ing riv - ers through the south-land's ver - dant door. She's ___
glides a - long the wood - land, through the hills and by the shore. Hear the

might - y tall and hand - some, and ___ known quite well by all. She's the
might - y rush of en - gine and the lone - some whis - tle's call;

reg' - lar com - bi - na - tion of the Wa - bash Can - non - ball.

THE WELLS AND FARGO LINE

1. Come lis - ten to my sto - ry, I'll not de - tain you
2. Oh, there was Ma - jor Thomp - son, turned up the o - ther

long, A - sing - ing and a - hum - ming__ this__ sim - ple__ sil - ly
day, He said that he would hold them up or the de - vil would be to

song. 'Tis of the old ex - con - victs, the men who served their
pay. For he could hold a ri - fle and draw a bead so

time For rob - bing moun - tain stag - es on the__ Wells and Far - go line.
fine U - pon those shot - gun mes - sen - gers of the Wells and Far - go line.

3. And there was Jimmy Miner who thought he was a thief,
   But he did surely prove himself to be a dirty sneak;
   And now behind San Quentin's walls he's serving out his time,
   For giving tips to old Jim Hughes on the Wells and Fargo line.

4. And there was still another who well did play his part;
   He's known among the mountains as the highwayman, Black Bart.
   He'd ride the trail both night and day
   For the Wells and Fargo treasure.

5. And now my story's ended, I've not detained you long,
   A-singing and a-humming this simple silly song.
   And though the nights are long, boys, and weary grows the time,
   But when we are out we'll ride again the Wells and Fargo line.

WHEN THE CURTAINS OF THE NIGHT
ARE PINNED BACK

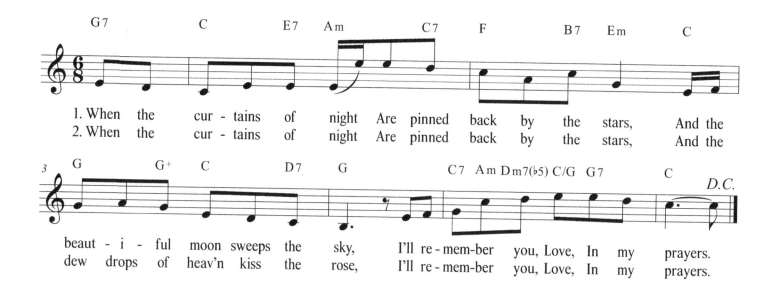

1. When the cur - tains of night Are pinned back by the stars, And the
2. When the cur - tains of night Are pinned back by the stars, And the

beaut - i - ful moon sweeps the sky, I'll re - mem - ber you, Love, In my prayers.
dew drops of heav'n kiss the rose, I'll re - mem - ber you, Love, In my prayers.

WHEN THE WORK'S ALL DONE THIS FALL

4. His body was so mangled the boys all thought him dead,
   They picked him up so gently and laid him on a bed;
   He opened wide his blue eyes and looking all around
   He motioned to his comrades to sit near him on the ground.
   "Boys, send my mother my wages, the wages I have earned,
   For I am afraid, boys, my last steer I have turned.
   I'm going to a new range, I hear my Master's call,
   And I'll not see my mother when the work's all done this fall.

5. "Bill, you may have my saddle; George, you may take my bed;
   Jack may have my pistol, after I am dead.
   Boys, think of me kindly when you look upon them all,
   For I'll not see my mother when the work's all done this fall."
   Poor Charlie was buried at sunrise, no tombstone at his head,
   Nothing but a little board and this is what it said,
   "Charlie died at daybreak, he died from a fall,
   The boy won't see his mother when the work's all done this fall."

THE YELLOW ROSE OF TEXAS

1. There's a yel - low rose of Tex - as I'm go - in' for to see, No
2. Where the Ri - o Grande is flow - ing and star - ry skies are bright, She
3. Oh,___ now I'm goin' to find her, my heart is full of woe; We'll

oth - er sol - dier knows her, no - bo - dy on - ly me. She cried so when I left her, it
walks a - long the riv - er in the qui - et sum - mer night. She thinks if I re - mem - ber we
sing the song to - geth - er we___ sang so long a - go. We'll play the ban - jo gai - ly and

like to broke my heart, And___ if I e - ver find her,___ we
part - ed long a - go; I___ prom - ised to come back a - gain and
sing the songs of yore, And the yel - low rose of Tex - as will be

ne - ver more will part She's the sweet - est rose of co - lor this sol - dier ev - er knew. Her
nev - er let her go.
mine for - ev - er - more.

eyes are bright as dia - monds, they spar - kle like the dew. You may talk a - bout your win - some maids and

sing of Ros - a - lie, But the yel - low rose of Tex - as beats the belles of Ten - nes - see. ___

YI-PEE-TY-EE I'M OFF TO TRUCKEE

WORDS & MUSIC by Rich Hinrichsen

THE ZEBRA DUN

1. We were camped up-on the plains at the head of the Cim-ar-ron When a-
2. We asked if he'd had break-fast, but he had-n't had a sniff. We
3. A-bout the Span-ish war and fight-ing on the seas With
4. Such an ed-u-cat-ed fel-ler, his thoughts just came in herds; He as-

long came a stran-ger and he stopped to ar-gue some. He
o-pened up the chuck box and told him to help him-self. He
guns as big as steers and ram-rods big as trees, And a-
ton-ished all them punch-ers with his jaw-break-ing words. He

looked so ver-y fool-ish, we be-gan to look a-round; We
took a cup of cof-fee, some bis-cuits and some beans, And
bout old Paul Jones, a mean, fight-ing son of a gun, Who
just kept on a-talk-ing till he made the boys sick, And

thought he was a green-horn just es-caped from town.
then be-gan to talk a-bout for-eign kings and queens.
was the grit-tiest cuss that e-ver pulled a gun.
they be-gan to fig-ure up some way to play a trick.

5. He said he had lost his job
   upon the Santa Fe
   And was going across the plains
   to strike the 7-D.
   He didn't say how come it,
   some trouble with the boss,
   But said he'd like to borrow
   a nice fat saddle hoss.

6. This tickled all the boys to death,
   they laughed way down in their sleeves,
   "We will lend you a horse just
   as fresh and fat as you please."
   Shorty grabbed a lariat
   and roped the Zebra Dun
   And turned him over to the stranger
   and waited for the fun.

7. Old Dunny was a rocky outlaw
     that had grown so awful wild
   That he could paw the white out
     of the moon every jump for a mile.
   Old Dunny stood right still,
     as if he didn't know,
   Until he was saddled
     and ready for to go.

8. When the stranger hit the saddle,
     old Dunny quit the earth
   And traveled right straight up
     for all that he was worth.
   A-pitching and a-squealing,
     a-having wall-eyed fits,
   His hind feet perpendicular,
     his front ones in the bits.

9. We could see the tops of the mountains
     under Dunny every jump,
   But the stranger he was growed there
     just like the camel's hump;
   The stranger sat upon him
     and curled his black mustache
   Just like a summer boarder
     waiting for his hash.

10. He thumped him in the shoulders
      and spurred him when he whirled,
    To show them flunky punchers
      that he was the wolf of the world.
    When the stranger had dismounted
      once more upon the ground,
    We knew he was a thoroughbred
      and not a gent from town;

11. The boss who was standing round
      watching of the show,
    Walked right up to the stranger
      and told him he needn't go,
    "If you can use the lasso like
      you rode old Zebra Dun,
    You are the man I've been looking for
      ever since the year one."

12. Oh, he could twirl the lariat
      and he didn't do it slow,
    He could catch them fore feet nine out
      of ten for any kind of dough.
    There's one thing and a shore thing
      I've learned since I've been born,
    That every educated feller
      ain't a plumb greenhorn.

Index of First Lines

Glossary

abandonado	abandoned
arroyos	steep-sided gully
bridle	headgear used to control a horse, consisting of buckled straps to which a bit and reins are attached.
brogan shoes	Brogan-like shoes, called "brogues" were made and worn in Scotland and Ireland as early as the 16th century.
bronco	untamed horse
buckaroo	cowpuncher
bummer	nickname of American Civil War foragers of Sherman's army during its March to the Sea and beyond
cavvy	herd of horses from which a cowboy selects his mount for the day.
chaparral	vegetation consisting chiefly of tangled shrubs and thorny bushes
chaps	leather pants without a seat, worn by a cowboy over ordinary pants to protect the legs.
Cheyenne	capital city of Wyoming
chico	boy
cholla	cactus with a cylindrical stem, native to Mexico and the southwestern US.
chuck	food
cocinero	cook or chef
coin the money	hand out otherwise worthless tokens and have people accept them as worth real things
corral	pen for livestock
corrido	ballad in traditional Mexican style
cucaracha	cockroach
curlew	large wading bird of the sandpiper family, with a long down-curved bill, brown streaked plumage, and frequently a distinctive ascending two-note call.
cut a mount	separate a horse from a herd
dan	mother horse (dam)
Dead March	march played by a military band at military funerals and executions
dogies	cattle
dram house	saloon
dun	horse with a dark colored stripe running along the spine from withers to tail (called a dorsal stripe) and a body that is a much lighter shade of that stripe
fiery	another word for paint

flume	artificial channel conveying water
get tight	tendency to get mean and disagreeable
gin-sot	one who is stupefied by drink
greenhorn	novice cowboy
hack	type of horse used for riding out at ordinary speeds over roads and trails
Hangtown	At one point, during California's Gold Rush, Placerville was called Hangtown because of the numerous hangings that took place in the town.
hatful blind	bet all the money without looking at the cards
hoolihan	backhand loop thrown with a lariat
horn	prominent projection on top of the pommel of a saddle
hoss	horse
jag	bout of unrestrained activity or emotion, especially drinking, crying, or laughing
kak	saddle
Kansias	Kansas
lit a shuck	left in haste for another location
Llano	treeless grassy plain
lowing	ordinary vocal sounds made by cattle
mañanitas	mornings
mount	horse
nag	small or sprightly horse or pony; by extension any horse, especially an old or over-worked horse
outlaw	horse that was spoiled in breaking
paint	pinto
pall	heavy cloth draped over a coffin
Pecos	river in SW United States
picket pin	long metal or wooden stake, often with a swiveling ring on the top, used for tethering a horse in an open area
rabble soldier	rebel soldier during Civil War
remuda	string of riding horses
round-up	gathering of horses or cows
sabe	knows
scrub races	horse race
Shenandoah	John Skenandoa, an elected chief of the Oneida
snuffy	buff- or snuff-colored horse
stampede	sudden, frenzied rush or headlong flight of a herd of frightened animals

stirrup	device attached to a horse's saddle that forms a loop with a flat base to support a rider's foot
stray	animal that has wandered away from a herd or off its home range.
tenderfoot	newcomer to the cowboy life; also known as a "greenhorn"
vaquero	cowpuncher
wrangler	man who cares for and outfits saddle horses
zebra dun	dun with dark stripes or bars on its legs
zephyr	soft gentle breeze.

Alternative Titles and Roud Number

Table. The Roud number is used to uniquely identify a folk song, regardless of its title. This is helpful because some folk songs go by many different titles. The initials n.a., meaning "not applicable," are used when a folk song has no Roud number. Data source: The Vaughan Williams Memorial Library (https://www.vwml.org/).

Song title	Alternative titles	Roud number
El Abandonado		n.a.
Across the Wide Missouri	Cross The Wide Missouri, Heaving The Lead, Oh Shangadore, River Shenandore, Rollin' River, Rolling River, Rolling-river, Salladore, Shanadar, Shanadar, Shanadoah, Shanadore, Shanadore Capstan Chanty, Shanandore, Shanandore, Shanendoah, Shangadore, Shannador, Shenandoah, Shenandore, Snenandoah, The Wide Missouri, Wide Missouri, The Wide Mizzoura, The Wild Missouri, The Wild Miz-zou-rye	324
The Big Corral	Get Along to the Big Coral	24611
Billy The Kid		5097
Blood on the Saddle	The Bloody Cowboy, There's Blood on the Saddle, Trail End	3685
Buffalo Gals	Ain't Ya Comin' Out Tonight, Alabama Gal, Alabama Gal, Alabama Gals Ain't You Coming Out Tonight, Alabama Girl Ain't You Comin' Out Tonight, Bowery Boys, Bowery Gals, Buck Creek Gals, Buck Creek Girls Won't Go to Somerset, Buffalo Gal, Buffalo Girl's Coming Out Tonight, Buffalo Girls, Buffalo Girls At Nome, Buffalo Girls Coming Out Tonight, Cincinnati Girls, Dance by the light of the moon, Jim Town Girls, Louisiana Gal, Louisiana Girls, Maxwell Girl, Maxwell Girls, Oh Lil Gal, Oh Lil' Gal, Old Aunt Katy Won't You Come Out Tonight, Philadelphia Gals Will You Come Out Tonight, Round Town Girl Won't You Come Out Tonight, Round Town Girls, Roundtown Gals, Roundtown Girls, St. Helena Girls, The Lushbaugh Girls, West Virginia Girls, Won't You Come Out, Won't You Walk Out Tonight	738

Song title	Alternative titles	Roud number
The Buffalo Hunters	Boggus Creek, Boggy Creek, Buffalo Range, Buffalo Skinners, Canaday-i-o, Craigle's Buffalo Hunt, Hills of Mexico, Murphy's Ranch, On the Hills of Mexico, Range of the Buffalo, Ranging Buffalo, The Buffalo Skinners, The Hills of Mexico	634
Bury Me Not on the Lone Prairie	Bury Me Not, Bury Me Not in the Deep Deep Sea, Bury Me Not on the Chickamauga, Cowboy's Lament, The Dying Cowboy, The Dying Cowboy's Prayer, The Lone Prairi, The Lone Prairie, The Lonesome Prairie, O Bury Me Not, O Bury Me Not in the Deep Blue Sea, The Ocean Burial, Oh Bury Me Not, Oh Bury Me Not on the Lone Prairie, Take Me Back to the Lone Prairie, The Texas Rangers	631
Chopo		8049
Cielito Lindo		25611
Cindy	The Ballad of Cindy, Beefsteak, Beefsteak When I'm Hungry, Cindy in the Summertime, Get Along Home Cindie, Get Along Home Cindy, Get Along Home Miss Cindy, Get Along Home Miss Lizie, Get Along Sindy, Git Along, Git Along Cindy, Git Along Miss Cindy, Kiss Me Cindy, Liza Jane, The Privates Eat the Middlin', Run Along Home With Lindy, Sindy	836
The Colorado Trail	Colorado Trail	6695
Corrido de Kiansis I		n.a.
Corrido de Kiansis II		n.a.
Cowboy Jack	Cow-boy Jack, He Was Just a Lonely Cowboy, Jack Was a Lonely Cowboy, Jack's a Lonely Cowboy, Just a Lonely Cowboy, Your Sweetheart Waits For You Jack	3244
Cowboy Lullaby		n.a.
The Cowboy	The Biblical Cowboy, Cow Boy Carol	5102
The Cowboy's Lament	A Western Cowboy, As I Walked Out in the Streets of Laredo, Big Kid's Barroom, Come Carry Me to Prairie, Cow Boy, Cowboy, The Cowboy, Cowboy Song, Cowboy in White Linen, Cowboy's Lament, Dying Cowboy, The Dying Cowboy, The Dying Shellback, Gambling Blues, In the Streets of Laredo, Jack Combs, Jack Combs's Death Song, John Sherman's Barroom, Laredo, Lidian Barroom, The Lineman's Hymn, Old Joe's Barroom, Old	23650

Song title	Alternative titles	Roud number
	Laredo, Soldier Shot in the Wrong, St. James's Hospital, St. Thomas's Hospital, The Streets of Hamtramck, Streets of Laredo, The Streets of Laredo, Take Me to the Graveyard and Place the Sod O'er Me, Those Gambler's Blues, Tom Sherberner's Barroom, Tom Sherman's Barroom, Way Down in Lodora, The Western Cowboy, The Wild Cowboy, The Wild Lumberjack, William Cook, Willie Brooks, The Young Cowboy, Young Cowboy	
La Cucaracha		n.a.
The Days of '49	The Days of Forty-nine, In the Days of Forty-nine	2803
Down in the Valley	Birmingham Jail, Birmingham Jail No.2, Down in Those Valleys Down Below, Down in those Valleys, Give My Heart Ease, Leopold Jailhouse, The Shreveport Jail, Willie My Darling	943
The Dreary, Dreary Life	A Cowboy's Life, Border Ballad, Come Along All You Cowboys, The Cowboy's Life, Cowboy's Life is a Dreary Dreary Life, The Cowboy's Life is a Very Dreary Life, The Dreary Life, The Kansas Line, The Lumberman's Life, The Pecos Stream, Shanty Boy, The Shanty Man, Shanty Man's Life, The Shanty-man's Life, The Shantyman's Life	838
The Dying Ranger	A Soldier's Farewell to West Constant, The Banks of the Potomac, Burma Soldier, Down in the Lone Star State, The Dying Cowboy, Dying Prisoner, Dying Ranger, The Dying Soldier, Dying Wisconsin Soldier, The Dying Wisconsin Soldier, The Lone Star State, Old New England, The Shades of the Palmetto, Soldier of Algiers, The Soldier's Farewell, The Sun Was Setting in the West, The Texas Ranger, The Wisconsin Soldier Boy	628
Git Along, Little Dogies	Get Along Little Dogies, Git Along Little Dogie, Go on You Little Dogies, Little Dogie, Roll on Little Doggies Roll on, Run Along You Little Dogies, Run Along You Little Dogies, Whoopee High Ogie, Whoopee Ti Yi Yo Git Along Little Dogies, Whoopee Ti-yi-yo. Roll on Little Dogies, Whoopee Ty Yi Oh Get Along Little Doggies, Whoopee to Yi Yo, Whoopie Ti Yi Yi Get Along Little Doggies	827

Song title	Alternative titles	Roud number
Goodbye, Old Paint	Chayanne, Cheyenne, Good-by Old Paint, Good-by Old Paint I'm Leavin' Cheyenne, Good-bye Old Paint, I Ride An Old Paint, I'm A-leaving Cheyenne, Leadin' Ole Paint, My Sweetheart's a Cowboy, Old Paint, Ride Old Paint, Ridin' Old Paint, Riding Old Paint Leading Old Bald, Sweet Lily	915
Ho! Westward Ho!		n.a.
Home on the Range	An Arkansas Home, Arizona Home, The Garbage Dispute, A Home on the Range, Home in the Hills, Home in the Sky, Home in the West, O Give Me a Home Where the Buffalo Roam, The Prospector's Home, Western Home	3599
I Ride an Old Paint	Chayanne, Cheyenne, Good-by Old Paint, Good-by Old Paint I'm Leavin' Cheyenne, Good-bye Old Paint, Goodbye Old Paint, I'm A-leaving Cheyenne, Leadin' Ole Paint, My Sweetheart's a Cowboy, Old Paint, Ride Old Paint, Ridin' Old Paint, Riding Old Paint Leading Old Bald., Sweet Lily	915
Jack o' Diamonds	Drunkard's Hiccoughs, The Drunkard's Hiccups, The Drunkard's Song, Jack Diamond, Peace and Content, A Card-player's Song, Ace and Deuce of Diamonds, Clinch Mountain, Drunken Hiccups, I am Travellin' to the Mountain, I am a Rebel Soldier, I'm Goin' to Build Me a Steeple, I'm Going to Georgia, Jack O' Dimons, Jack of Diamonds, Long Ways From Home, O Lillie O Lillie, Oh Molly, One Morning in May, The Rebel Prisoner, The Rebel Soldier, Red Whiskey, Rye Whiskey, Rye Whiskey Rye Whiskey, Squeeball, Sunny South, The Troubled Soldier, Way Up on Clinch Mountain	259
Jesse James	Frank and Jesse James, I Went Down to the Depot, Jessee James, Jessie James, Life and Death of Jesse James, Poor Jesse James, The Death of Jesse James, Twenty-one Years	2240
Little Joe, the Wrangler		1930
Lo Que Digo		n.a.
The Lover's Lament	As Time Draws Near, Banishment, Breast of Glass, Come Pity Me the Time Draws Nigh, Dearest Dear, Farewell, I Love You Well, My Dearest Dear, Oh Now to Me the Time Draws Near, Oh Unto Me the	3601

Song title	Alternative titles	Roud number
	Time Drew Near, Oh to Me the Time Draws Near, Oh to Me the Time Draws Nigh, Oh to Me the Time Grew Near, Oh to Me the Time Rolls Nigh, Parting Song, Queen Elender, The Breast of Glass, The Parting Lovers, The Time Draws Near, To Me My Love the Time Draws Nigh, When You and I Must Part, Woe Unto Me When the Time Draws Near, Woe Unto You the Time Has Come	
Las Mañanitas		n.a.
My Love Is a Rider	Beware of a Cowboy Who Wears a White Hat , Buckin' Bronco, Bucking Bronco, The Cowboy With the White Hat, The Cowboy's Hat, The Cowgirl My Love is a Cowboy, My Lover's a Cowboy, My Lover's a Rider	934
Night-Herding Song	Night Herding Song, The Night Herding Song, The Night-herding Song	4444
The Old Chisolm Trail	Old Chisholm Trail, Riding Round the Cattle, Chisholm Trail, Clear Rock's Chisholm Trail, Come Along Boys Listen to My Tale, Cow Cow Yicky Ticky Yea, Cow Cow Yiki, Eleven Slash Slash Eleven, Jimmie Tucker, The Last Time I Seen Her, Leadbelly's Chisholm Trail, Old Chis'olm Trail, The Old Chis'olm Trail, The Old Chizzum Trail, Out on the Western Plains, That'll Do Young Man, Western Cowboy, Western Plain, When I Was a Cowboy, When the Boys were Out on the Western Plains	3438
Old Dan Tucker	Big Tom Bailey, Dan Dan the Funny Wee Man, Dan Tucker, Dan'l Tucker, De Bran New Old Dan Tucker, De New Old Dan Tucker, Get Out De Way The Holland Song, Old Johnny Tucker, I Found a Horse Shoe, Ol' Dan Tucker, Old Ann Tucker, Old Man Tucker, Old Miss Wilson, Old Mister Tucker, Old Tom Wilson, Ole Bull and Dan Tucker, Ole Dan Tucker, Ole Tan Tucker, The Original Old Dan Tucker, Walk Tom Wilson	390
Old Texas	Going to Leave Old Texas, The Texas Song	12711
Poor Lonesome Cowboy	The Lonesome Cowboy	4643
The Railroad Corral	Railroad Corral	4636

Song title	Alternative titles	Roud number
Red River Valley	Bright Little Valley, The Bright Little Valley, The Bright Mohawk Valley, Bright Sherman Valley, Cowboy Love Song, The Cowboy Love Song, From the Valley You're Going, In the Bright Mohawk Valley, Laurel Valley, Little Darling, Little Lonely Valley, The Little Valley, Lost River Desert, The Red River Valley, Sherman Valley	756
Sam Bass	Young Sam Bass	2244
Sweet Betsy from Pike	Betsy From Pike, Betsy Mcpike, Isaac and Betsy, Sweet Betsy of Pike	3234
The Tenderfoot	Breaking in a Tenderfoot, D-2 Horse Wrangler, The D2 Horse Wrangler, The Horse Wrangler, Punching Cows, The Skewbald Black	3246
Tenting on the Old Campground	Tenting on the Old Camp-ground, Tenting Tonight, We're Tenting Tonight	14045
The Texas Rangers		480
El Toro Moro		n.a.
The Trail to Mexico	Following the Cow Trail, J.H. Stanton, The Mexico Trail, New Mexico, On The Trail To Mexico, The Trail of '83, The Year of '83, Trail To Mexico	23455
The Wabash Cannonball	Wabash Cannon Ball, The Wabash Cannon Ball, Wabash Cannonball	4228
The Wells and Fargo Line		11083
When the Curtains of Night Are Pinned Back	Curtains of Night, The Curtain of Night, The Curtains of Night, I'll Remember You Love, I'll Remember You Love in My Dream, I'll Remember You Love in My Prayer, I'll Remember You in My Prayers, I'll Remember You Love in My Prayers, I've Loved You So True, When the Curtains of Night	4367
When the Work's All Done This Fall	A Group of Jolly Cowboys, After the Roundup, The Cowboy, The Cow Puncher's Lament, Dixie Cowboy The Old Cow Puncher, When Work is Done This Fall	450
The Yellow Rose of Texas	E Yaller Rose Ob Texas, The Bouncing Girl in Fogo, The Girl From St. John's City, Yellow Rose of Texas	2800
Yipeetyee I'm off to Truckee		n.a.

Song title	Alternative titles	Roud number
The Zebra Dun	Ballad of the Old Zebra Dun, Educated Feller, Old Don, Old Zebra Dun, The Educated Feller, Zebra Dun, The Zebra Dunn	3237

References

Lomax, J.A. 1911. Cowboy songs and other frontier ballads. Sturgis & Walton Company, New York.

Lomax, J.A., and A. Lomax. 1934. American ballads and folk songs. Macmillan, New York.

Sandburg, C. 1927. The American songbag. Harcourt, Brace & Company. New York.

Metropolitan Museum of Art. 1991. Songs of the wild west. Metropolitan Museum of Art, Simon & Schuster books for Young Readers, New York.

Thorp, N.H. 1908. Songs of the cowboys. Houghton Mifflin Company, New York.

Tinsley, J.B. 1981. He was singin' this song : a collection of forty-eight traditional songs of the American cowboy, with words, music, pictures, and stories. University Presses of Florida, Orlando.

Tinsley, J.B. 1991. For a cowboy has to sing. University of Central Florida Press, Orlando.

Made in the USA
Columbia, SC
05 April 2019